Stories ca[ ] counted on!

Ideas for developing mathematics through story

Neil Griffiths

Stories can be counted on!

Published by

Corner To Learn Limited

Willow Cottage • 26 Purton Stoke

Swindon • Wiltshire SN5 4JF • UK

www.cornertolearn.co.uk

ISBN: 978-1-905434-18-3

Text © Neil Griffiths 2007

Photographs of Neil in action! © Lis McDermott 2007

First published in the UK 2007

Edited by Helen O'Neill

Design by David Rose

Photography by Lis McDermott

Illustrations by Doug Nash

Printed by Tien Wah Press Pte. Ltd., Singapore

Introduction

The aim of this book is to provide practitioners with ideas for developing mathematics using quality picture books and well-known rhymes. The book is intended for practitioners working with young children in early year settings and, of course, at home.

The National Numeracy Strategy (1999) indicated that *"… stories, rhymes and songs can be chosen which rely for their appeal on the pleasure of counting, the sequencing of events and the use of everyday words to describe position or direction."*

For mathematics to be relevant, young children need to be given meaningful, interesting, practical activities which stimulate them and encourage them to want to learn.

"Mathematical activities for young children must be within their experience of everyday life and must involve them in active exploration of the world around them."
(Planning for Progression. Inspection and Advisory Services, Wales.)

Children relate to books, their characters, experiences and storylines. These can often help children to relate to the world around them and it therefore seems a logical extension to use them as a source of activities and games to develop mathematical learning.

Using stories and rhymes for mathematics will provide:

- a context for learning
- relevance
- a clear purpose
- practical application
- visual reinforcement
- stimulus for wanting to learn
- enjoyment and fun

This book is intended to help practitioners to provide and structure a range of exciting mathematical activities and investigations using stories and rhymes as a starting point for exploration. Most activities use resources that can easily be found or are readily available in an Early Years setting. Each section will offer a different approach for using picture books, indicating preparation and resources, introducing activities, extension opportunities, key mathematical vocabulary to be introduced, a useful recommended book list and key Early Learning goals covered.

In addition to addressing all the learning goals for mathematics at both the Foundation stage and the early stages of the National Curriculum, the following learning goals will be explored in the book:

In personal, social and emotional development:

- continue to be excited and motivated to learn.
- be confident to try new activities, initiate ideas and speak in a familiar group.
- maintain attention, concentration and sit quietly when appropriate.
- respond to significant experiences, showing a range of feelings when appropriate.
- form general relationships.
- work as part of a group or class.

In language, communication and literacy:

- enjoy listening to and using spoken and written language.
- practise attentive listening.
- listen with enjoyment and respond to stories.
- extend their vocabulary.
- speak clearly.
- use language to imagine and recreate rules.
- use talk to organise sequence and clarify ideas.
- show an understanding of the elements of stories.

In knowledge and understanding of the world:

- investigate objects and materials by using all of their senses as appropriate.
- look closely at similarities, differences, pattern and change.
- ask questions about why things happen.

In physical development:

- move with confidence, imagination and safety.
- travel around, under, over and through equipment.
- show awareness of space.
- use a range of small equipment.

In creative development:

- explore colour, texture, shape, form and space on two and three dimensions.
- sing simple songs.
- use their imagination in role-play.

Let's sequence!

Using illustrations to develop sequencing and to encourage ordering skills

The ability to sequence and order is an important early skill for successful young mathematicians.

A story is a narrative and, by its nature, is therefore a series of events. Most stories therefore tend to follow a logical order or 'time line'. Picture books can provide wonderful opportunities for children to get involved in sequencing activities.

Preparation and Resources

Two copies of one book will be needed as there are usually illustrations on each side of a page. Cut the books up and create one set which shows the full sequence of the story as below.

> **❝** *Picture books can provide wonderful opportunities for children to get involved in sequencing activities.* **❞**

Cover the backs of each of these pages with blank paper to avoid children confusing which page is part of the sequence, and cover or erase each page number. You may also decide to cover the text with paper if you wish the children to sequence by picture clues alone.

Introductory Activities

Initially, offer the children two pictures to look at.

Ask questions such as these:

- Which comes first in the story?

- Which comes last in the story?

- Does this picture come before or after this one?

Extend the activity by adding more pictures to put in order. These can be hung on a washing line.

Encourage the children to talk about their decisions and give reasons for their ordering.

Ask questions such as these:

- Why are you placing this picture here in the sequence?

- Why does this picture come before this one?

- Why is this picture third in the sequence?

- Is this picture towards the beginning or the end of the sequence?

- Shall we place this picture to the left or right of this one?

Finally, when the children are confident with this activity, give them a whole story to sequence. The length of this story should match the children's ages and levels of ability.

Extension

- Make a collection of props from a story and ask the children to sequence them in the correct order of the storyline.

- Give a set of pictorial instructions, e.g. the route to the school office; how to plant a seed. Can the children follow the sequence?

- Make bead sequences on laces.

- Look at a simple recipe. Can the children remember what to do in the correct order? Finally, make the recipe.

- Place a set of objects on the table. Let the children look at them closely. Then cover the objects. Can they remember their correct order?

- Make repeating patterns using unifix, etc.
- Tell well-known stories and encourage the children to re-tell the story sequence.

Key Mathematical Vocabulary

First, second, third, …	1st, 2nd, 3rd, …
before, next to, after	order
sequence	place
last	beginning, end, middle
left, right	beside
last but one	before, after
next, between	

Recommended Book List

Balloon, Jez Alborough (Harper Collins)

The Bad-Tempered Ladybird, Eric Carle (Picture Puffin)

Ben and Gran and the Whole Wide World,
   Gillian Shields & Katherine McEwen (Macmillan)

The Enormous Turnip, Traditional (Ladybird)

Follow My Leader, Emma Chichester Clark
   (Harper Collins)

Jasper's Beanstalk, Mick Inkpen (Hodder and Stoughton)

The Journey, Neil Griffiths (Red Robin Books)

No room for a baby roo!, Neil Griffiths
   (Red Robin Books)

Someone Bigger, Jonathan Emmett &
   Adrian Reynolds (OUP)

The Tiger Who Came to Tea, Judith Kerr
   (Harper Collins)

Walter's Windy Washing Line, Neil Griffiths
   (Corner to Learn)

Walter's Windy Washing Line

by Neil Griffiths

Illustrated by Judith Blake

Key Early Learning Goals Covered

- Say and use number names in order in familiar contexts.

- Use developing mathematical ideas and methods to solve practical problems.

- Talk about, recognise and recreate simple patterns.

- Use everyday words to describe position.

Patterns, patterns everywhere!

Using illustrations to explore patterns and shape

> **We are fortunate in this country to have a wonderful collection of high-quality picture books.**

We are fortunate in this country to have a wonderful collection of high-quality picture books available through bookshops and libraries. These books contain outstanding illustrations that are colourful and eye-catching and provide excellent starting points for discussion and questions. In particular, these illustrations are often full of examples of shape, pattern, size and use of space.

Preparation and Resources

Make a collection of books that offer excellent illustrations and starting points for discussion. Big Books are more useful as a large group can then use the material at the same time, whilst smaller versions should be used for small group activities. You might like to cut up some books and laminate the illustrations for regular use.

Introductory Activities

- Allow the children to enjoy the illustrations.

- Encourage free discussion and careful observation.

- Use the illustrations for mathematical discussion and activities.

- For younger children, choose illustrations that are simple and uncluttered. For more able children, use more intricate illustration styles.

Ask questions such as these:

- How many stripy pants are there?

- Which pair of pants is the biggest?

- Which pair of pants is the smallest?

- How many spotty pants are there?

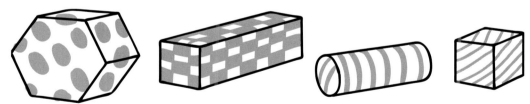

- Can you point to a square shape?

- Can you find a circle?

- What shape is this?

- What do you think is inside this parcel?

- How many parcels have spotty paper?

- What shape is the parcel that has a checked pattern?

Stories can be counted on! 13

Extension

- Ask the children to choose a favourite illustration and create their own simple questions for a friend.

- The children draw their own pictures for discussion.

- Explore wrapping paper designs together. They provide excellent opportunities for discussion.

Key Mathematical Vocabulary

long	longest	tall	
short	high	low	shape
pattern	curved	straight	round
solid	corner	2-D shapes	under
over	above	below	top
bottom	in front	next to	beside

Recommended Book List

Barty's Ketchup Catastrophe, Sally Chambers (Myriad)

Bear in a Square, Stella Blackstone (Barefoot Books)

My Mum and Dad Make me Laugh, Nick Sharratt (Walker Books)

Pants, Giles Andreae & Nick Sharratt (Random House)

Pass the Jam, Jim, Kaye Umansky (Red Fox)

The Queen's Knickers, Nicholas Allan (Random House)

Shapes, Robert Crowther (Walker Books)

The Tiger Who Came to Tea, Judith Kerr (Harper Collins)

The Very Hungry Caterpillar, Eric Carle (Picture Puffin)

Count on us!

Using illustrations as a starting point and stimulus for counting and number activities

"Illustrations in picture books provide the child with a visual challenge."

All children love to count, particularly if there is a context and clear purpose for the activity. Illustrations in picture books provide the child with a visual challenge and can make counting and number work relevant and fun.

Preparation and Resources

Make a collection of books that have illustrations with potential for counting activities within them. Big Books are more useful as large groups can then access the material at the same time, whilst smaller versions should be used for small group work. You might like to cut up some books and laminate useful illustrations for regular use.

Introductory Activities

Choose simple illustrations for younger children and more complex styles for older pupils.

- Allow the children to enjoy the illustrations.
- Encourage free discussion and careful observation.
- Use the illustrations for mathematical discussion and activities.

The cottage is soon restored to its original beauty ...

... and that afternoon the villagers enjoy a delicious and colourful afternoon tea.

Examples of questions that might be asked about this illustration:

- How many birds can you see?

- How many people at the party are wearing something with stripes on?

- How many people can you see standing up?

- If four people went home early, how many would be left?

- If six more people joined the party, how many people would there be?

- If there are four cherry cakes on each plate, how many would there be on five plates?

Extension

Using illustrations in this way involves questioning, and it will be important that children clarify and seek clear explanations from the teacher.

How often does a teacher say, "Do you all understand?" Everyone nods that they do, even though five minutes later a child reveals they don't in fact understand! This is a natural reaction as children are often nervous of appearing confused in front of peers or a teacher.

This activity should seek to encourage children to make sure they fully understand a question, so the teacher should encourage the children to ask for clarification.

Example:

Teacher: How many cherry cakes can you see?

The child should be encouraged to ask:

Child: Are they cherry cakes or strawberry cakes in the picture?

Teacher: How many people can you see wearing hats?

Child: Is a scarf a hat?

The children should also be encouraged to set their own questions about an illustration for friends to answer.

Key Mathematical Vocabulary

number	zero, one, two …	none
how many	count	count to
count back	more, less	many
odd	even	pair
first, second …	add	subtract
double	difference	

Recommended Book List

The Baby's Catalogue,
   Janet Ahlberg (Puffin)

Cockatoos, Quentin Blake
   (Red Fox)

The Great Pet Sale, Mick Inkpen
   (Hodder and Stoughton)

Kipper's Toybox, Mick Inkpen
   (Hodder and Stoughton)

*Mrs McTats and her houseful
   of Cats*, Alyssa Satin Capucilli
   (Pocket Books)

Mrs Rainbow, Neil Griffiths
   (Red Robin Books)

No room for a baby roo!, Neil Griffiths
   (Red Robin Books)

The Tiger Who Came to Tea, Judith Kerr
   (Harper Collins)

The Very Hungry Caterpillar, Eric Carle (Picture Puffin)

Key Early Learning Goals Covered

- Say and use number names in order in familiar contexts.

- Count reliably up to 10 everyday objects.

- Use developing mathematical ideas and methods to solve practical problems.

- In practical activities and discussion, begin to use vocabulary involved in adding and subtracting.

- Use language such as 'more' or 'less' to compare two numbers.

- Find one more or one less than a number from 1 to 10.

- Begin to relate addition to combining two groups of objects, and subtraction to 'taking away'.

Words, words, words!

Stories as a rich source of mathematical vocabulary in context

It is extremely important that the young mathematician learns the 'language' and 'vocabulary' of the subject as soon as possible. Stories with an exciting storyline provide a useful context for introducing vocabulary. The task for the teacher is to draw out important mathematical language from the story and offer it for discussion, role-play and practical activity.

Preparation and Resources

Make a collection of books which are rich in mathematical vocabulary or provide a context within their storyline for encouraging discussion and the use of mathematical language.

Examples:

*The **little** mouse chose the **biggest piece** of cheese and had almost eaten **half** of it when the cat pounced!*

*There were **three tiny** fish **in** the **round** aquarium and a **fat** cat sitting **on** a fur rug. **Next to** the cat was a cage **full** of **long**, sleeping snakes!*

> **"***The task for the teacher is to draw out important mathematical language.***"**

21

> **"It is important that the enjoyment of a story is not spoilt by regular interruptions."**

It is important that the enjoyment of a story is not spoilt by regular interruptions. Therefore, enjoy the story fully first. Then return to the story and focus on the mathematical vocabulary.

Follow this sequence:

- Say the word.
- Read it again in context.
- Ask the children, 'What does this word mean?'
- Use a practical, real-life example to reinforce its meaning.
- Offer an additional practical activity to cement the children's understanding of the word.

Examples:

Kipper counted all his toys again into the basket: 'One, two, three, four, five, six, seven!' He had one more toy this time! (From *Kipper's Toybox* by Mick Inkpen.)

- Focus on *counted*.
- Focus on *one more*.
- Provide the children with a real basket of toys.
- Count to six. Then add a toy.
- Count to seven.
- Explore *one more*.
- Extend to 'two more'. Then other numbers.

Having read the story of *The Three Bears,* focus on the table that has been laid for breakfast. Using role-play equipment, set out a table for the three bears. Whilst the text has only limited mathematical vocabulary, the context of the story provides an excellent opportunity for additional counting and the introduction of language associated with size, shape, position, order, capacity, etc.

Talk about vocabulary associated with:

shape:	round, square, rectangular, etc.
size:	long, big, small, etc.
order:	longest, biggest, smallest, etc.
position:	behind, above, left of, next to, etc.
capacity:	full, empty, half full

Extension

- Encourage the children to look for mathematical vocabulary in a story.

- Make up a story together and include mathematical vocabulary.

- Make a maths dictionary together.
- Role-play mathematical stories in the role-play area, in water or in sand.

Examples of useful stories for this purpose:

The Enormous Turnip, Traditional (Ladybird)

Five Little Ducks, Ian Beck (Orchard Books)

The Shopping Basket, John Burningham (Picture Lion)

Ten in the Bed, Penny Dale (Walker Books)

Recommended Book List

Bear In a Square, Stella Blackstone (Barefoot Books)

Big, David Bedford (Little Hare)

Goldilocks and the Three Bears, Tony Bradman
(Methuen)

Kipper's Toy Box, Mick Inkpen (Hodder and Stoughton)

Little Bear's Little Boat, Eve Bunting (Bloomsbury)

Sometimes I Like to Curl up in a Ball, Vicki Churchill
& Charles Fuge (Gullane Children's Books)

We're Going on a Bear Hunt, Michael Rosen and
Helen Oxenbury (Walker Books)

Where is Spot? Eric Hill (Picture Puffin)

Key Early Learning Goals Covered

- Say and use number names in order in familiar contexts.

- Use language such as 'more' or 'less' to compare two numbers.

- Use language such as 'greater', 'smaller', 'heavier', 'lighter' to compare quantities.

- Use language such as 'circle' or 'bigger' to describe the shape and size of solids and flat shapes.

- Use everyday words to describe position.

Transformers!

Enjoying stories that contain transformations in size, shape and distance

Children will thoroughly enjoy the following collection of stories that deal with changes in shape, size and distance.

Blue Balloon
Mick Inkpen

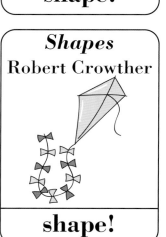

shape!

Baabooom!
Martin Waddell

size!

Tiny
Paul Rodgers
& Korky Paul

distance!

Shapes
Robert Crowther

shape!

The Very Hungry Caterpillar
Eric Carle

size!

What's the time Grandma Wolf?
Ken Brown

distance!

Extension

- Explore the changing shapes and sizes of balloons.

- Examine the growth of plants.

- Make a 'watercress head' and watch the hair grow!

- Hatch caterpillars in the classroom.

- Look at pictures of the children as babies and notice how they have transformed.

- Measure heights of children.

Key Mathematical Vocabulary

measure	size	guess
compare	length, width	height, depth
long, short, tall	wide, narrow	longest, shortest
far, near	weigh	heavy, light
big	small	large
tiny, huge	bigger, smaller	

Key Early Learning Goals Covered

- Use language such as 'greater', 'smaller', 'heavier', 'lighter' to compare quantities,

- Use language such as 'wide' or 'bigger' to describe the shape and size of solids and flat shapes.

Count on stories!

Stories that count

A vast choice of picture books can now be collected that encourage and include counting in their storylines. Many are highly original and eye-catching, motivating the reader to enjoy counting as a meaningful, useful and fun activity.

Preparation and resources

It can be great fun seeking out picture books that involve counting. There are many to choose from and it will be important to select those that appeal to children through original storylines, clever rhyming and high quality illustrations. In some, counting is an integral part of the text, whilst others encourage the child to count through more subtle storylines.

Introductory Activities using Counting Books

- Simply enjoy the story.
- Encourage the children to join in.
- Use fingers to represent numbers as you count.

- Ask the children to point at the illustrations and physically count.

- Mime, role-play and use sound effects to support the counting, e.g:

  one leopard: (the children roar and hold up 'claws')
  two elephants: (they trumpet and hold up 'trunks')
  three monkeys: (they make monkey noises and scratch)

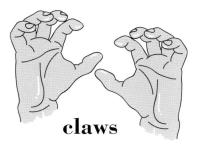

claws

trunk

monkey noises

- Encourage the children to use their hands in response to a story.

millipede

butterfly

caterpillar

snail

spider

worm

- Create sets of cards that match an item or items counted in the story. (These will have to be drawn or painted by an adult or child. For copyright reasons, they must not be photocopied.)

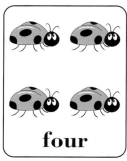

one

two

three

four

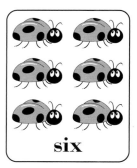

five

six

These can then be used in a whole variety of number activities, including:

- say and use numbers in order

- recite the number names in order

- count backwards and forwards from a given number

- count up to 10 objects

- recognise numerals 1 to 9

- recall numbers

- use language such as 'more', 'less', 'greater', 'smaller' to compare two numbers

- order a set of numbers

- begin to understand and use ordinal numbers
- begin to use the vocabulary involved in adding and subtracting

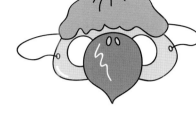

- Create masks to support the counting activities in a storyline.
- Collect props that match those in the story. The children can both role-play with them and count them physically.

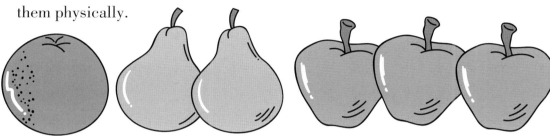

Count to ten

The following is a list of books that will help children recognise and understand numbers from 1 to 10.

1 *One Pink Pig*, Sandy Nightingale (Picture Puffin)
One Bear All Alone, Caroline Bucknall (Macmillan)

2 *Mr Magnolia*, Quentin Blake (Red Fox)
Alfie's Feet, Shirley Hughes (Red Fox)

3 *The Three Pigs* (Traditional)
Goldilocks and the Three Bears, Tony Bradman (Methuen)

4 *Four Black Puppies*, Sally Grindley (Walker Books)

5 *Five Little Ducks*, Ian Beck (Orchard Books)

6 *Six Dinner Sid*, Inga Moore (MacDonald)

7 *Sixes and Sevens*, John Yeoman & Quentin Blake (Picture Mac)

8 *?*, Do you have any examples?

31

9   *Nine Ducks*, Sarah Hayes (Walker Books)

10   *Ten Sleepy Sheep*, Holly Keller (Hippo)

     Ten in the Bed, Penny Dale (Walker Books)

     Ten Tiny Ants, Rosemary Reville Irons (Kingscourt)

Key Mathematical Vocabulary

number	one, two …	zero
1st, 2nd …	first, second …	count
odd	even	pair
pattern	add, more	subtract, less
double	how many	take away
one less	one more	different

Recommended Book List:

**for stories that use counting as
an integral part of the story**

1, 2, 3 to the Zoo, Eric Carle (Hamish Hamilton)

The Bad Babies Counting Book, Tony Bradman
   (Beaver Books)

One Duck, Another Duck, Charlotte Pomerantz &
   Jose Aruego (Picture Puffin)

One Pink Pig, Sandy Nightingale (Picture Puffin)

Ten in the Bed, Penny Dale (Walker Books)

Ten, Nine, Eight, Molly Bang (Picture Puffin)

Ten Sleepy Sheep, Holly Keller (Hippo)

Ten Tiny Ants, Rosemary Reville Irons (Kingscourt)

We all went on Safari, Laurie Krebs & Julia Cairns
   (Barefoot Books)

Recommended Book List:

for stories that include counting as a subtle element of the storyline

Cocatoos, Quentin Blake (Red Fox)

The Doorbell Rang, Pat Hutchins (Picture Puffin)

The Enormous Turnip, Traditional (Ladybird)

Five Little Ducks, Ian Beck (Orchard Books)

Four Black Puppies, Sally Grindley (Walker Books)

Grandma Brown's Three Fine Pigs, Neil Griffiths
   (Storysack)

Handa's Surprise, Eileen Browne (Walker Books)

Kipper's Toy Box, Mick Inkpen (Hodder and Stoughton)

Mrs McTats and her Houseful of Cats,
   Alyssa Satin Capucilli (Pocket Books)

Six Dinner Sid, Inga Moore (Macdonald)

The Shopping Basket, John Burningham (Picture Lion)

The Very Hungry Caterpillar, Eric Carle
   (Picture Puffin)

Grandma Brown's Three Fine Pigs
by Neil Griffiths

Illustrated by Judith Blake

More than just a good story

Picture books with a subtle focus on a mathematical operation

"...it can be an overwhelming task choosing appropriate material for use with children."

Before beginning this section, it is important that practitioners not only choose stories for their potential in developing mathematics, but should also ensure that they are a good story to begin with.

Such is the enormous variety of picture books currently available, that it can be an overwhelming task choosing appropriate material for use with children. A useful guideline is to ask these questions before choosing a book:

- Does it have a good storyline? (i.e. interesting content, fast moving, an introduction that makes the reader curious and a good ending which leaves the reader laughing or crying, thoughtful and satisfied.)

- Is it a memorable storyline?

- Are the illustrations appropriate for the age of the child, (i.e. not too detailed for young children), eye-catching colourful and bright?

- Is the content suitable for young children?

- Does the story have strong, recognisable and memorable characters?

- Is it original in its approach and does it have additional features that add to the attraction of the book? (i.e. flaps, holes, feely bits, noises, etc.)

The focus in some stories is a mathematical operation and this can be an excellent vehicle for introducing children to a new area of mathematics, providing context, relevance, purpose and visual reinforcement. The children will be stimulated by the story and therefore enjoy their learning.

See pages 68–72 for a list of books and the mathematical operations and areas of mathematics they introduce. It can be clearly seen that the whole of the Foundation Stage for mathematics and Early Learning goals can be introduced through story.

Where shall we start?

Using picture books as a context for learning in mathematics

"Picture books … provide an excellent starting point for mathematical study."

Teachers often look for exciting ways to introduce new mathematical topics, e.g:

- the ticking of a collection of clocks to introduce time
- a pizza to introduce 'half' and 'quarter'
- food packaging to introduce 3-D shape
- ribbons to introduce length.

Picture books can also provide an excellent starting point for mathematical study. Whilst the stories themselves may not be particularly mathematical, they can introduce the children to a topic that can then be used for mathematical study, e.g. *Itchy Bear* by Neil Griffiths. This enchanting story about a bear could be the starting point for 'Teddy bear Maths'. The children could bring in their own teddies from home and then the maths fun can begin, e.g:

- tallest bear
- data
- ordering bears
- heaviest bear
- sorting bears
- largest bear
- teddy bear shop money
- counting bears

36

- pattern and shape
- bear pairs
- oldest / youngest bear

The following is a list of stories and the starting points they can offer for mathematical exploration and investigation.

Handa's Surprise, Eileen Brown – Fruit Maths

Kipper's Toy Box, Mick Inkpen – Toy maths

Five Little Ducks, Traditional – Duck maths

Mrs McTats and her Houseful of Cats, Alyssa Satin Capucilli – Cat maths

Six Dinner Sid, Inga Moore – Pet maths

The Tiger Who Came to Tea, Judith Kerr – Teatime maths

Balloon, Jez Alborough – Balloon maths

Jessie's Flowers, Ron Bacon – Flower maths

Mrs Lather's Laundry, Allan Ahlberg & Andre Amstutz – Clothes maths

Spot's Birthday Party, Eric Hill – Birthday maths

Alfie's Feet, Shirley Hughes – Body maths and Shoe maths

My Cat Likes to Hide in Boxes, Eve Sutton & Lynley Dodd – Boxes maths

Pants, Giles Andreae & Nick Sharratt – Underwear maths

Introductory Activities

- Read the story as a starting point.

- Expand on the topic covered, e.g. talk about toys.

- Ask the children what they know about the subject. (What toys do they have? How do they work?)

- Ask the children to bring in items from home.

- Make a collection of items.

- Match your planning to the items available.

Examples:

Topic

2-D shape: Explore shape of toys.

Sorting: Sort toys by materials, e.g. plastic, wood, metal.

Addition: Use a collection of toys in a toy box to 'add one' and 'take one away'.

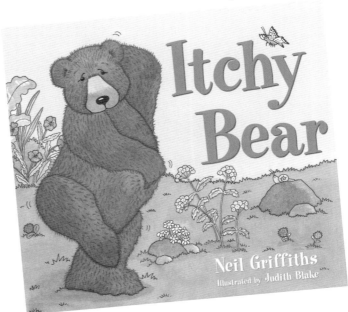

The following two examples illustrate how a picture book can be used as a starting point for mathematical investigation.

The Shopping Basket,
John Burningham (Picture Lion)

What you need
A nice shopping basket filled with the following items for each catagory:

Shape:	3-D packages, e.g. Toblerone®, Oxo® cubes, toothpaste box, tin cans, balls
Area:	wrapping paper, greeting cards
Length:	string, laces, ribbon
Capacity:	different plastic bottles
Mass:	rice, cotton wool, dog biscuits, pasta
Multiplication/ Sharing:	multi-packs, Oxo® cubes, cheese spread portions
Fractions/Sharing:	chocolate bars, chocolate orange
Counting:	Smarties®, dog biscuits

Let the investigations begin!
Using the book and shopping basket you can now explore:

Number:	counting, addition, subtraction, 'one less', 'one more', sharing
Matching:	animal to items, animals to places
Sequencing:	food items, places visited
Shape:	food items in rubbish basket
Capacity:	full, empty basket
Pattern:	patterns of food items
Sorting:	sort food by: round, not round; fruit, not fruit, etc.
Data:	bar graph of items in basket; bar graph of children's favourite foods in basket

Stories can be counted on!

Oliver's Fruit Salad and Oliver's Vegetables

Vivian French (Hodder Children's Books)

What you need

A collection of real or plastic fruit and vegetables.

Let the investigations begin!

With the fruit and vegetables you can now explore the following activities:

Number:	context for number rhymes, e.g. one potato, five little peas, four scarlet berries
	counting
	estimating: Ask, *How many (carrots) are in the bag?*
	one more than
	one less than
	ordinal numbers: Ask, *Which fruit is (third) in the line?* Children place fruit and vegetables in order.
	addition
	subtraction
Creating patterns:	e.g. sequencing with fruit and vegetables
Matching:	e.g. different fruit and vegetables; varieties of the same fruit e.g. Cox apples together
Sharing:	e.g. pieces of fruit and vegetables
Sorting:	e.g. by shape, colour, variety, pip, no pip, stone, no stone, rolls, won't roll, round, not round, shiny, not shiny, etc.
Money:	Ask questions, e.g. *How much for three apples at 1 pence each?*
Fractions:	e.g. cutting fruit into halves and quarters

Measuring:	e.g. measuring length of runner beans, carrots, etc.
	long, short, round, thin, fat
Mass:	e.g. weighing fruit and vegetables,
	heavy, light, heaviest, lightest
Estimating:	Ask questions, e.g. *How many peas weigh one pound / kilogram?*
Direction/ position:	Place fruit on a tray and ask the children to describe its position, e.g. *The apple is next to the pear. The orange is to the right of the cherries.*
	Also put vegetables in sand tray for this activity.
Time:	Days of the week
Shape:	Use feely bags and ask, *What fruit can you feel?*
	Is any fruit symmetrical?
	round, long, flat
Data handling:	e.g. bar charts of favourite fruit and vegetables, etc.

Stories can be counted on!

My mathematical day!

"*… the re-telling of simple daily events can be a source of mathematical study.*"

Children regularly arrive at school and have stories to tell about what has happened at home during the evening, weekend or holidays. These stories and the re-telling of simple daily events can be a source of mathematical study. For example:

- A walk to school can lead to discussion about shape and pattern in nature, routes and directions.

- Snack time can lead to talking about halves and quarters.

- Bathtime can offer opportunities to talk about 'empty'.

The following timetable is of a typical day and the 'mathematical stories' that can be woven into discussion. The teacher may also make a collection of items to support practical investigations, e.g. a collection of clothes or socks for 'getting dressed' or a collection of litter for 'walking home'.

Stories can be counted on

My mathematical day

1 Getting up
time, day of the week, date

2 Getting dressed
counting, sorting, matching clothes, pairs of socks

3 Having breakfast
capacity: empty, full – milk cartons, bowls, cups
shape: cereal boxes, tins, plates, bowls, cups, saucers
matching position: laying the table
fractions: half, quarter, whole – piece of toast

4 The journey to school on the bus
routes
direction
positional vocabulary – describe the journey
timetables
money for fare
queuing at the bus stop
counting people on the bus
ordinal numbers

5 Snack time
fruit pieces – half, quarter
sharing

6 Lunch (packed lunch)
items in lunch box: shape, length, fractions, mass,
counting, capacity, sharing
data – favourite lunches

Stories can be counted on!

7 Walking home through the park
collecting leaves
picking up litter
shape, counting, sorting, sets, size, capacity

8 Shopping
shopping basket: counting, size, shape, sharing, add,
subtract, money
measures: length, mass
capacity
data: favourite food

9 Tea time
cooking meal: planning, estimation, mass, capacity,
    time of cooking, sharing out mixture
laying table: counting, position, matching, sorting

10 Playing games and phoning a friend
associated skills
number: telephone numbers

11 Bath time
capacity: bath filling
counting: bath toys

12 Bedtime story
associated skills

Additional ideas: playing with toys, journey by train, gardening,
visit to the park, in the car, washing the car, washing clothes

The following is a list of stories that could accompany exploration of 'a mathematical day'. They will provide a further context for study. Teachers might choose to return to 'a mathematical day' throughout the year or build it into termly planning.

My mathematical day – Stories to accompany activities

1 *Time to Get Up*, Gill Mclean (Tamarind)
   Terrible Tuesday, Hazel Townson and Tony Ross
      (Beaver Books)

2 *Alfie's Feet*, Shirley Hughes (Red Fox)

3 *Don't Forget the Bacon*, Pat Hutchins
      (Picture Puffin)

4 *Rosie's Walk*, Pat Hutchins (Picture Puffin)
   The Wheels on the Bus, Paul Zelinsky
      (Dutton Books)
   Ready, Steady, Go, Shigeo Watanabe (Red Fox)

5 *Eat up, Gemma*, Sarah Hayes and Jan Ormerod
      (Walker Books)
   The Giant Jam Sandwich, John Vernon Lard and
      Janet Burroway (Macmillan Children's Books)

6 *Six Dinner Sid*, Inga Moore (MacDonald)

7 *Percy the Park Keeper*, Nick Butterworth
      (Harper Collins Children's Books)

8 *Teddybears Go Shopping*, Susanna Gretz and
      Alison Sage (A & C Black children's books)

Maths market!

Creating role-play to encourage mathematical exploration

Role-play and role-play areas, both indoors and outdoors, are a crucial part of any Early Years setting. Play is the world and work of a young child and the most effective way for a child to learn. It therefore seems obvious that such play will encourage communication and, of course, story telling. The role of the teacher will be to listen and observe this play and to intervene at the appropriate time to extend and enhance learning opportunities.

Role-play areas can be excellent starting points for learning across the whole curriculum.

A role-play area that can be re-visited on a regular basis is a 'Maths Market' or 'Maths Shop'. In the market, each shelf can be designed to encourage exploration of different areas of the maths curriculum.

Activities

The market has been designed to represent all aspects of maths – from measures to multiplication and from sharing to shape. Each shelf is devoted to a theme, and cards

"Play is the world and work of a young child..."

suggest activities and introduce important vocabulary. Although the market can be used independently by children in their free play, it is designed for use by small groups accompanied by an adult who directs learning.

Time: clocks, sand timers, stopwatches, watches

Shape: 3-D packaging e.g. Toblerone® (triangular prism), etc. The market is decorated with 2-D shapes for the children to identify.

Area: wrapping paper and greetings cards

Length: balls of string, ribbons, laces

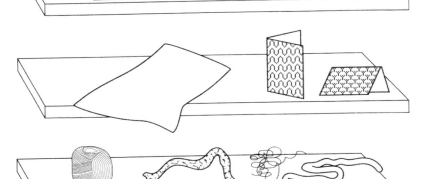

Capacity: plastic bottles of different sizes – full, empty, half-full

Weight: packages of varying weight, e.g. rice, pasta, dog biscuits

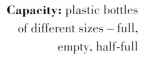
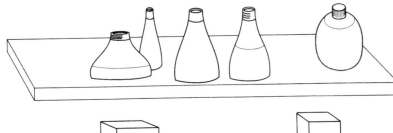
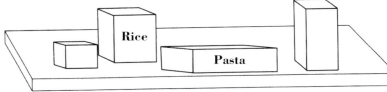

Stories can be counted on

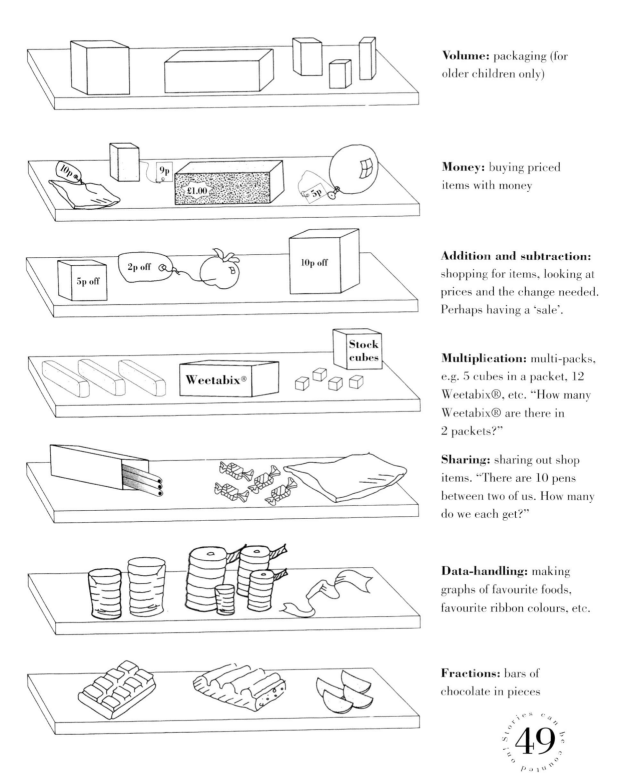

Volume: packaging (for older children only)

Money: buying priced items with money

Addition and subtraction: shopping for items, looking at prices and the change needed. Perhaps having a 'sale'.

Multiplication: multi-packs, e.g. 5 cubes in a packet, 12 Weetabix®, etc. "How many Weetabix® are there in 2 packets?"

Sharing: sharing out shop items. "There are 10 pens between two of us. How many do we each get?"

Data-handling: making graphs of favourite foods, favourite ribbon colours, etc.

Fractions: bars of chocolate in pieces

49

Let's go on a journey!

Exploring journeys in stories

"Stories often follow a journey..."

Stories often follow a journey, providing opportunities for activities on routes, directions, mapping and positional vocabulary.

Preparation and Resources

- A collection of books that allow young children to follow the journey within a story. Excellent examples are:
  Rosie's Walk, Pat Hutchins (Picture Puffin)
  We're Going on a Bear Hunt, Michael Rosen and Helen Oxenbury (Walker Books).

Introductory Activities

- Read the story.

- Talk about the journey the characters followed.

- Draw the journey together on large sheets of paper with big pens or with chalk on a tarmac surface. At first, the children will need a lot of help.

- Create the journey in the sand tray and add small-world props.
- Collect large props and role-play outfits and act out the journey.

On the following two pages are two examples of 'journey' maps that can be copied to accompany *Rosie's Walk* and *We're Going on a Bear Hunt*.

Sensory Experiences

Allow the children to create a sensory journey, e.g. roll in grass, splash water, snap twigs, squelch in mud, feel ice, hide in the dark.

Extension

- Allow the children to create their own simple maps from a story.
- Give the children an imaginary map and encourage them to make up their own story to accompany the map.
- Go on a real journey.
- Follow treasure trails.
- Go on a paper chase.

Rosie's Walk – Base Mat

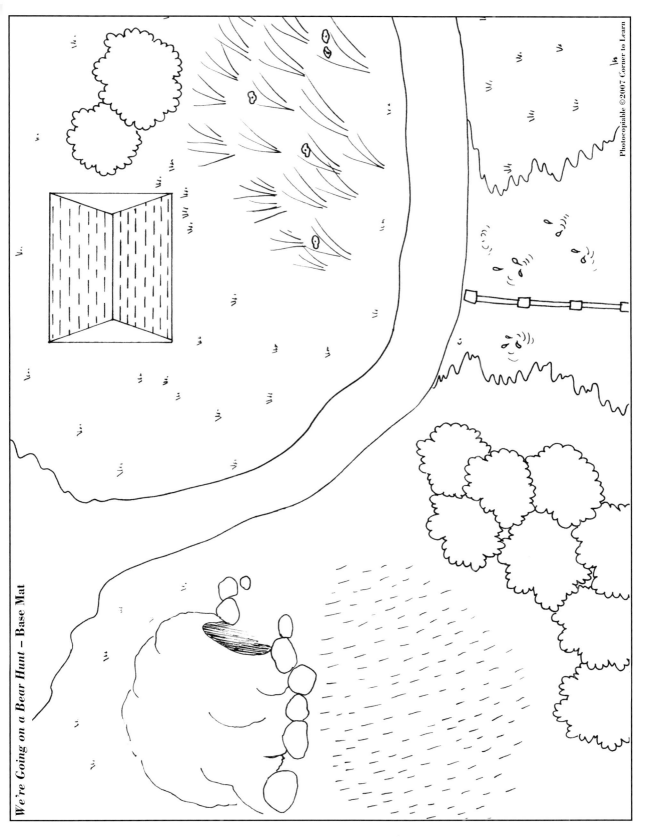

We're Going on a Bear Hunt – Base Mat

Recommended Book List

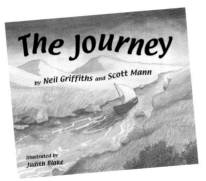

The Journey
by Neil Griffiths and Scott Mann
Illustrated by Judith Blake

Nursery rhymes

Nursery rhymes are a delightful starting point for number work and many rhymes include counting. The value of rhyme work in developing children's use of language, speech and listening skills is enormous. They are also, of course, great fun.

The following is a list of rhymes and songs that encourage counting.

Nursery rhymes – including number

This Little Puffin, Elizabeth Matterson (Puffin Books)

This little pig went to market (5)
One man went to mow
One potato, two potato
One, two, three, four, five
One finger, one thumb, keep moving
Round and round the garden (2)
Two fat gentlemen met in a lane
Two little blackbirds sitting in the sun
Two little dicky-birds sitting on a wall
Two little eyes to look all around
Baa baa black sheep (3)
Hickory Dickory Dock (3)
Three jellyfish, three jellyfish
Three little monkeys were jumping on the bed
Four little fishes swimming in the sea
Four scarlet berries

"*Nursery rhymes are a delightful starting point for number work…***"**

There were five little snowmen
There were five little spacemen
I know an old lady (5)
Build a house with five bricks (5)
Five brown eggs in a nest of hay
Five cherry cakes in a baker's shop
Five currant buns in a baker's shop
Five fluffy chicks
Five hot cross buns in a baker's shop
Five little candles
Five little ducks went swimming one day
Five little froggies sitting on a wall
Five little leaves so bright and gay
Five little mice came out to play
Five little peas in a pea-pod pressed
Five little sparrows I can see
Five mince pies in a baker's shop
Five small stars that shone so bright
Five tall soldiers standing in a row
Five wood-pigeons sitting on a wall
This old man, he played one (10)
John Brown met a little Indian (10)
Ten fat sausages sizzling in the pan
Ten (five) green bottles, hanging on a wall
Ten little letters in a brown sack
Ten little squirrels sat on a tree
Ten wiry sparklers
There were ten in the bed
The twelve days of Christmas

Stories can be counted too!

Finger Puppets

You may copy these patterns to make finger puppets to accompany the singing and role-play of well-known rhymes.

Basic Shape

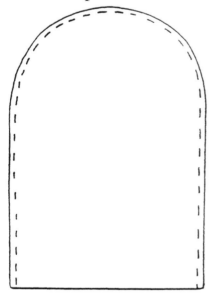

Mouse

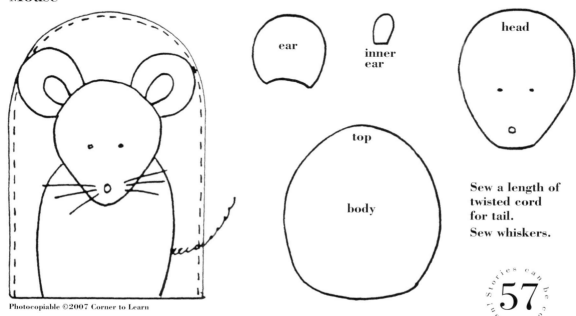

ear

inner ear

head

top

body

Sew a length of twisted cord for tail.
Sew whiskers.

Teddy Bear

Frog

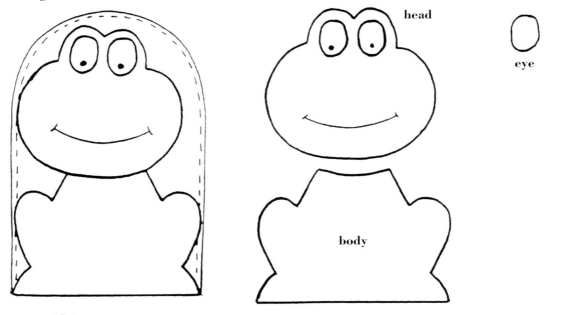

Stories can be counted on!

Monkey

face

body

arm

arm

inner
ear

Spider

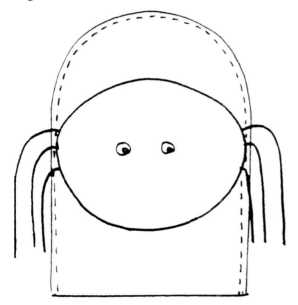

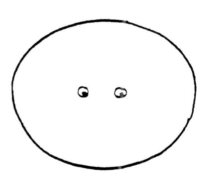

Use fur fabric for spider's body.
Sew lengths of wool for legs.
Glue on wobbly eyes.

Stories can be counted out

Soldier

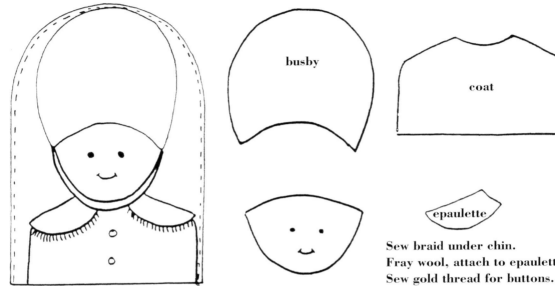

busby

coat

epaulette

Sew braid under chin.
Fray wool, attach to epaulette.
Sew gold thread for buttons.

King

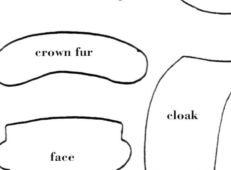

crown

neck fur

crown fur

cloak

cloak

face

Sew sequins on crown.

Stories can be counted out!

Queen

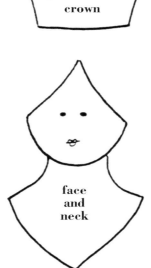

crown

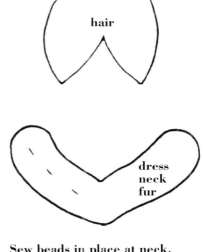

hair

face
and
neck

dress
neck
fur

Sew beads in place at neck.
Sew sequin/bead on crown.

Farmyard – sheep

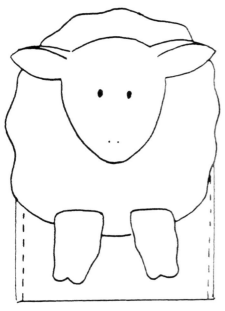

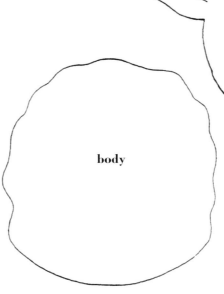

body

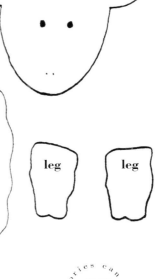

leg   leg

Stories can be counted on!

Farmyard – farmer

hat

head

body

beard

Cut beard from
fur fabric.

coat

Farmyard – dog

body

ear x2

paw

paw

tail

Stories can be counted on!

Farmyard – cat

Sew whiskers.

tail

bib

body

paw paw

Farmyard – pig

body

leg leg

nose ear ear

Make tail from a length of twisted cord.

Stories can be counted on!

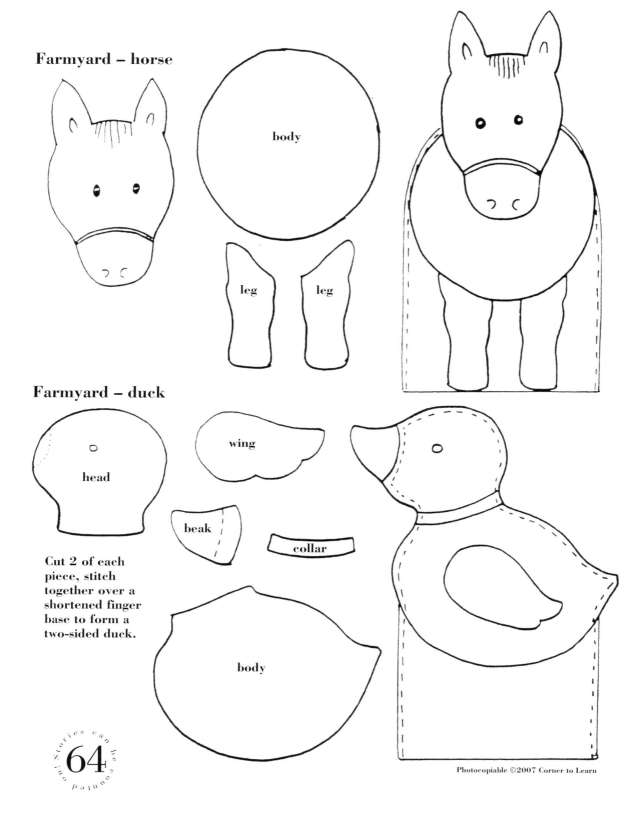

Farmyard – horse

body

leg leg

Farmyard – duck

head

wing

beak

collar

Cut 2 of each
piece, stitch
together over a
shortened finger
base to form a
two-sided duck.

body

Farmyard – goat

leg

hair

beard

body

horn

Farmyard – hen

Cut 2 of each piece, stitch together over a shortened finger base to form a two-sided hen.

tail

C

C

D

D

B

B

A

A

wing

Farmyard – cow

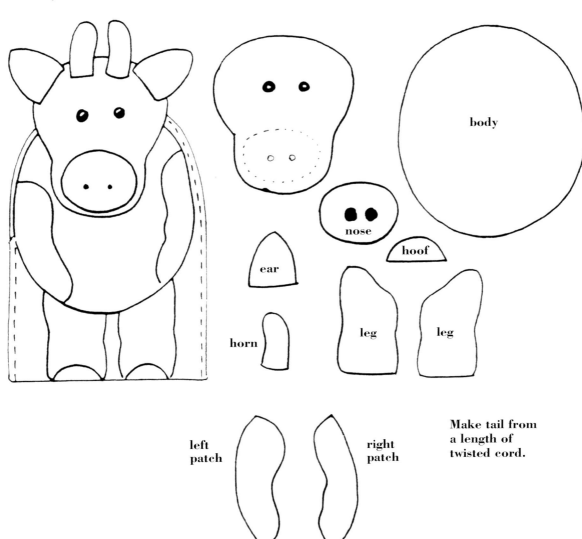

body

nose

ear

hoof

horn

leg

leg

left
patch

right
patch

Make tail from
a length of
twisted cord.

Conclusion

I hear, I forget.

I see, I remember.

I do, I understand.

If I enjoy it and can see a purpose,

I'll probably want to do it again!

Neil Griffiths

Maths Stories Booklist

Book Title	Author	Publisher	Maths Areas Covered
Number			
1, 2, 3 to the Zoo	Eric Carle	Hamish Hamilton	Counting
A Fishy Counting Story	Joanne & David Wylie	Franklin Watts	Counting (more or less than)
A Squash and a Squeeze	Julia Donaldson	Macmillan Children's Books	Problem-solving
Big Red Bath	Julia Jarman	Orchard Books	Addition and Subtraction
Billy's Beetle	Mick Inkpen	Hodder & Stoughton	Begin to understand vocab of addition & subtraction
Centipede's 100 Shoes	Tony Ross	Andersen	Counting to 50 (pairs)
Cockatoos	Quentin Blake	Red Fox	Counting to 10
Counting on an Elephant	Jill MacDonald	Picture Puffin Books	Counting
Cushie Butterfield	Colin McNaughton	Collins	One more
Duckies Ducklings	Francis Barry	Walker Books	Counting to 10
Fergus's Big Splash	Tony Maddox	Piccadilly Press	Addition and Subtraction
Five Little Ducks	Ian Beck	Orchard Books	Concept of 'less one'
Four Black Puppies	Sally Grindley	Walker Books	Number Story
Goldilocks and the Three Bears	Tony Bradman	Methuen	Counting (1–3)
Grandma Brown's Three Fine Pigs	Neil Griffiths	Storysack	Counting to 10
Handa's Hen	Eileen Browne	Walker Books	Counting to 10
Handa's Surprise	Eileen Browne	Walker Books	Ordinal Numbers, Subtraction
Kipper's Toy Box	Mick Inkpen	Hodder & Stoughton	Counting (within 15)
Jingle Jangle Jungle	Axel Scheffler	Campbell	Counting
Jump In	Ian Whybrow	Hodder & Stoughton	Addition
Meanies	Joy Cowley	E J Arnold	Counting
Mr Magnolia	Quentin Blake	Red Fox	Pairs (odd/even)
Mrs McTats and her Houseful of Cats	Alyssa Satin Capucilli	Pocket Books	Counting to 26
My Arctic 1 2 3	Michael Avvaaluk Kusagak	Annick Press Ltd	Counting
One to Ten and Back Again	Nick Sharratt	Puffin	Counting
One Bear all Alone	Caroline Bucknall	Macmillan	Counting
One Duck, Another Duck	Charlotte Pomerantz & Jose Aruego	Picture Puffin Books	Counting (1–10)
One Hunter	Pat Hutchings	Picture Puffin Books	Counting (1–10)
One Little Teddy Bear	Mark Burgess	Picture Puffin Books	Add and subtract from one number
One More Sheep	Mij Kelly	Hodder & Stoughton	One more
One Pink Pig	Sandy Nightingale	Picture Puffin Books	Counting
One, Two, Three, Oops	Michael Coleman	Myriad Books	Counting
One, Two, Three Jump	Penelope Lively & Jan Ormerod	Puffin	Counting
Please don't chat to the Bus Driver	Shen Roddie	Bloomsbury	Subtraction/Addition
Six Dinner Sid	Inga Moore	MacDonald	Counting to six
Sixes and Sevens	John Yeoman & Quentin Blake	Macmillan Children's Books	Counting

Someone Bigger	Jonathan Emmett & Adrian Reynolds	Oxford University Press	Ordinal Numbers, Sequencing
Teddybears	Susanna Gretz	Picture Lions	Counting (1–10)
Ten in the Bed	Penny Dale	Walker Books	Counting (1–10)
Ten Little Rubber Ducks	Eric Carle	Harper Collins	Ordinal Numbers
Ten Little Mice	Joyce Dunbar	Red Wagon Books	Tens
Ten Sleepy Sheep	Holly Keller	Hippo	Counting
Ten Tiny Ants	Rosemary Reville Irons	Kingscourt	Recite numbers in order, forwards/backwards
Ten, Nine, Eight	Molly Bang	Picture Puffin Books	Counting (1–10)
The Bad Babies Counting Book	Tony Bradman	Beaver Books	Counting
The Boy who was Followed Home	Margaret Mahy	Dutton Children's Books	Counting and Adding
The Doorbell Rang	Pat Hutchins	Picture Puffin Books	Number Story (factors of 12)
The Enormous Turnip	Traditional	Ladybird	Ordinal Number, Size
The Farm Concert	Story Chest	Nelson	Recite number names in order from 0–6
The Most Amazing Hide/ Seek Counting Book	Robert Crowther	Viking Kestrel	Counting (1–100)
The Nickle Nackle Tree	Lynley Dodd	Puffin Books	Counting and Adding
The Red Woollen Blanket	Bob Graham	Walker Books	Area
The Shopping Basket	John Burningham	Picture Lions	Counting and Subtracting
The Teddy Bears' Picnic	Jimmy Kennedy	Blackie	Estimating numbers in the range
The Three Little Pigs	Valerie Michant	Xylopress	Counting, comparing and ordering numbers
The Tiger who came to Tea	Judith Kerr	Collins	Begin to understand and use ordinal numbers
The Very Hungry Caterpillar	Eric Carle	Picture Puffin Books	Counting, Days, Ordering, Size, Length, Symmetry
We all went on Safari	Laurie Krebs & Julia Cairns	Barefoot Books	Counting
Witches Four	Marc Brown	Picture Corgi	Counting (4), Number story

Measuring & Weight

Big	David Bedford	Little Hare	Area/Size
Big and Small	David Bedford	Little Hare	Area/Size
Charlie Chick	Nick Denchfield	Campell Books	Size
Flat Stanley	Jeff Brown	Magnet	
Growing Frogs	Vivian French	Candlewick Press	Comparative Vocabulary/Measures
Jim and the Beanstalk	Raymond Briggs	Picture Puffin Books	Size, Need to measure, Scale for older children
Lengthy	Syd Hoff	World's Work	
Little Bear's Little Boat	Eve Bunting	Bloomsbury	Size
Mary Mary	Sarah Hughes & Helen Craig	Walker Books	Vocabulary related to length, Comparisons
Meg on the Moon	Jan Pienkowski	Picture Puffin Books	
Mrs Pepperpot	Alf Proyser	Young Puffin	
One-Eyed Jake	Pat Hutchins	Bodley Head Children's Books	Heavier, Lighter, Balance
Pardon? Said the Giraffe	Colin West	Walker Books	Comparative sizes
Peepo!	Janet and Allan Ahlberg	Picture Puffin Books	

Pig's Prize	Simon Puttock	Egmont	Size
Tall Inside	Jean Richardson	Picture Puffin Books	Size
The Bad Babies Counting Book	Tony Bradman	Beaver Books	
The Shrinking of Treehorn	Florence Parry Heide	Young Puffin	
The Teeny Weeny Tadpole	Sheridan Cain	Little Tiger	Size
The Trouble with Elephants	Chris Riddell	Walker Books	Size, Weight
Titch	Pat Hutchinson	Picture Puffin Books	Size
What's the time, Grandma Wolf?	Ken Brown	Andersen Press	Distance
Where's My Teddy	Jez Alborough	Walker Books	Concept of size
Who sank the Boat?	Pamela Allen	Puffin	Comparing size and weight of different animals
You'll Soon Grow into Them, Titch	Pat Hutchins	Red Fox	Vocabulary related to length, Comparisons

Time

Alfie Gives a Hand	Shirley Hughes	Picture Lions	
Balloon	Jez Alborough	Harper Collins	Sequencing
Clocks and More Clocks	Pat Hutchins	Picture Puffin Books	Time story
Cluck O'Clock	Kes Gray	Hodder	Telling time
Duck in a Truck	Jez Alborough	Harper Collins	Sequencing
Five Minutes' Peace	Jill Murphy	Walker Books	Passage of time
Follow my Leader!	Emma Chichester Clark	Collins	Order, Sequencing, One more, One less
Grandpa	John Burningham	Cape	Passage of time
Happy Birthday Sam	Pat Hutchins	Picture Puffin Books	Size and passage of time
I Want to see the Moon	Louis Baum	Magnet	
I went to the Zoopermarket	Nick Sharratt	Hippo	Sequencing
Jessie's Flowers	Ron Bacon	Shortlands	Time, Day & night sequencing
Just a Minute	Anita Harper	Picture Puffin Books	Minutes
Mr Wolf's Week	Colin Hughes	Picture Puffin Books	Days of the week
Mrs Lather's Laundry	Allan Ahlberg & Andre Amstutz	Puffin	
Next Please	Ernst Jandl and Norman Junge	Red Fox Books	One less
On Friday Something Funny Happened	John Prater	Picture Puffin Books	
Spot's Birthday Party	Eric Hill	Picture Puffin Books	
Sunshine	Jan Ormerod	Picture Puffin Books	Time Picture Book
Terrible Tuesday	Hazel Townson/Tony Ross	Beaver Books	Days of the week
The Bad Tempered Ladybird	Eric Carle	Picture Puffin Books	Size and reading of time
The Owl who was afraid of the Dark	Jill Tomlinson	Young Puffin	
The Time it took Tom	Nick Sharratt & Stephen Tucker	Scholastic Press	Time, Days, Weeks, Months
Time to get Up	Gill McLean	Tamarind	Days of the week, Time
What's the Time Dracula?	Victor G Ambrus	Oxford University Press	Dracula worries about a dentist's appointment at 3 o'clock

What's the Time Mr Wolf?	Colin Hawkins	Picture Lions	Time (clock)
When I was your Age	Ken Adams	Macdonald Young Books	Grandpa boasts about 'when he was Sammy's age'

Shape and Space

A Fishy Size Story	Joanne & David Wylie	Franklin Watts	Language for large
Alfie's Feet	Shirley Hughes	Red Fox	Left/Right, Right/Wrong, Pairs
Barty's Ketchup Catastrophe	Sally Chambers	Myriad	Shape
Bear in a Square	Stella Blackstone	Barefoot Books	Shape
Hoorah for Fish	Lucy Cousins	Walker Books	Pattern and Shape
I know a Rhino	Charles Fuge	Gullane Children's Books	Shape
If At First You Do Not See	Ruth Brown	Anderson Press	Puzzle Book
If You Look Around You	Fulvio Testa	Anderson Press	
Inside, Outside, Upside Down	Stan & Jan Berentain	Collins	Positional language
Jerry's Trousers	Nigel Boswall	Macmillan	Shape and Pattern
Marvin wanted More	Joseph Theobald	Bloomsbury	Vocabulary of size
My Cat Likes To Hide In Boxes	Eva Sutton & Lynley Dodd	Picture Puffin Books	Solid shapes
My Mum and Dad Make me Laugh	Nick Sharratt	Walker Books	Pattern
Oliver finds his Way	Phyllis Root	Walker Books	Direction and positional vocabulary
Pants	Giles Andreae & Nick Sharratt	Random House Children's Books	Pattern
Queenie the Bantam	Bob Graham	Walker Books	Direction, Positional vocabulary, Sequencing
Rosie's Walk	Pat Hutchins	Picture Puffin Books	Positional language
Ruby Flew Too	Jonathan Emmett	Macmillan	Positional, Vocabulary
Shapes	Robert Crowther	Walker Books	Shape
Snow White	Traditional	Various	
Sometimes I Like to Curl up in a Ball	Vicki Churchill & Charles Fuge	David & Charles Children's Books	Shape & Positional Vocabulary
Square Sweets That Look Round Charlie and the Chocolate Factory	Roald Dahl	Allen & Unwin Ltd	
The Boy With Square Eyes	Julien and Charles Snape	Julia Macrae Books	
The Hedgehog Mirror	Eva Marder	Abelard-Schuman Ltd	
The Journey	Neil Griffiths	Red Robin Books	Positional vocabulary, Direction, Sequencing
The Patchwork Quilt	Valerie Flournoy	Picture Puffin Books	
The Shopping Expedition	Andre Amstutz & Allan Ahlberg	Walker Books	Position & Direction (Shape)
The Queen's Knickers	Nicholas Allan	Random House Children's Books	Shape and Pattern
The Quilt	Ann Jonas	Picture Puffin Books	Dimensions
Wayne's New Shape	Calvin Irons	Kingscourt	Solid shapes
We're Going On A Bear Hunt	Michael Rosen	Walker Books	Position, Direction and Movement
What Colour are your Knickers?	Sam Lloyd	Gullane Children's Books	Sequencing, Pattern, Shape
When The Bears Came	Martin Waddell	Walker Books	Vocabulary describing position, Size, Data-handling

Stories can be only counted

Capacity

Come Away From The Water, Shirley	John Burningham & Jonathan Cape	Red Fox	
Mr Archimede's Bath	Pamela Allen	Bodley Head	
Thank You For A Drink Of Water	Patricia & Victor Smeltzer	Lion Books	
Tiddalick, The Frog Who Caused A Flood	Robert Roennfeldt	Picture Puffin Books	

Data

Eat Up Gemma	Sarah Hayes & Jan Omerod	Walker Books	Sorting, Data-handling
Farmer Duck	Martin Waddell	Walker Books	Data-shandling
Some Of Us	Ljiljana Rylands	Dinosaur	Sorting
The Baby's Catalogue	Janet Ahlberg	Puffin	Sorting and Grouping

Money

Dogger	Shirley Hughes	Red Fox	Money
Don't Forget The Bacon	Pat Hutchins	Picture Puffin Books	
Grandma Goes Shopping	Ronda and David Armitage	Picture Puffin Books	
Master Money The Millionaire	Allan Ahlberg	Puffin	Money
Teddybears Go Shopping	Susanna Gretz	Hippo	
The Great Pet Sale	Mick Inkpen	Hodder Children's Books	
The Shopping Basket	John Burningham	Picture Lions	

Fractions

Gumboots Chocolatey Day	Mick Inkpen	Macmillan	Fractions
Pog Climbs Mount Everest	Peter Haswell	Walker Books	Pog carries a ladder up a mountain, half way up, two and a quarter attempts
To Bed…or Else	Ewa Lipniacka	Magi Publications	Fractions expand the time, two, two and a half

Miscellaneous

Ben & Gran & the Whole Wide World	Gillian Shields & Katherine Mc Ewen	Macmillan Children's Books	Sequencing, Ordering, Distance
Duck in the Truck	Jez Alborough	Harper Collins	Sequencing
Ruby Flew Too!	Jonathan Emmett	Macmillan Children's Books	Direction
Sometimes I like to curl up in a ball	Vicky Churchill & Charles Fuge	Gullane Children's Books	Direction and Measures
The Pea and the Princess	Mini Grey	Red Fox	Shape, Area, Number, Measures, Pattern
The Noisy Farm	Marni McGee	Bloomsbury	Sequencing
Walter's Windy Washing Line	Neil Griffiths	Corner to Learn	Whole Maths Curriculum

Stories can be counted on